Copyright © 2024 Jennifer Jones
All copyright laws and rights reserved. Published in the U.S.A.
For more information, email info@ninjalifehacks.tv
Paperback ISBN: 978-1-63731-885-0 Hardcover ISBN: 978-1-63731-887-4
eBook ISBN: 978-1-63731-886-7

Find the Toys on Strike lesson plans at ninjalifehacks.tv

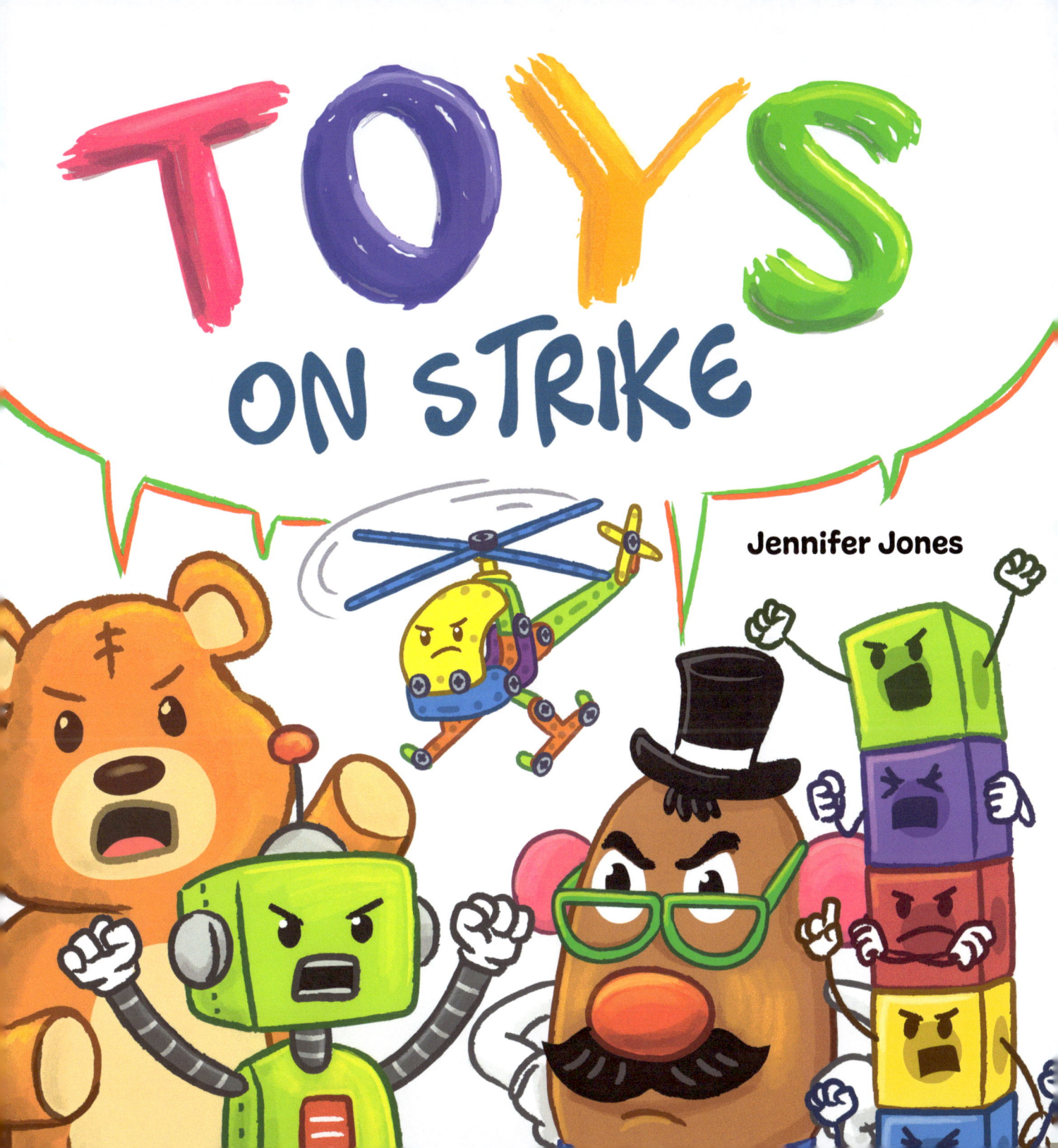

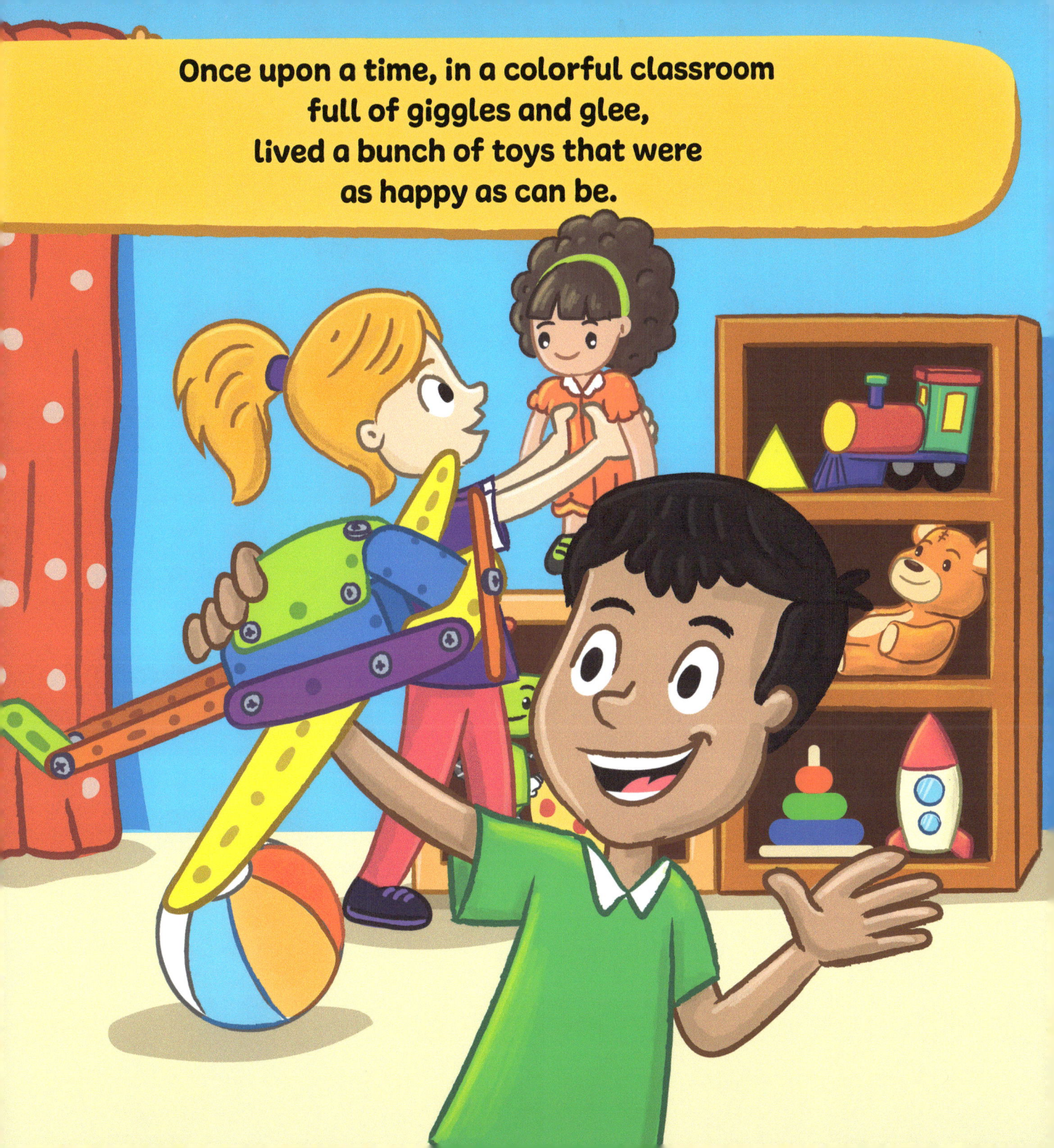

Once upon a time, in a colorful classroom full of giggles and glee, lived a bunch of toys that were as happy as can be.

One day, during playtime,
the toys had a chat.
They decided it was time
to fix all of that.

They wrote a letter to the students
to make it clear,
to explain their feelings
as they shed tears.

www.ingramcontent.com/pod-product-compliance
Lightning Source LLC
Chambersburg PA
CBHW041714160426
43209CB00018B/1834